SECOND FIGHT FOR INDEPENDENCE

# THE
# WAR
OF
# 1812

Charging across open ground, tightly packed British
ranks dissolve in the murderous fire from the American
line at the Battle of New Orleans on January 8, 1815.

SECOND FIGHT FOR INDEPENDENCE

# THE
# WAR
## OF
# 1812

ALDEN R. CARTER

## FRANKLIN WATTS
New York ★ Chicago ★ London ★ Toronto ★ Sydney
A First Book

# ACKNOWLEDGMENTS

Many thanks to all who helped with *The War of 1812: Second Fight for Independence*, particularly Don Beyer, Lorna Greenberg, Georgette Frazer, Barbara Feinberg, Brian Cain, Dean Markwardt, and my mother, Hilda Carter Fletcher. As always, my wife, Carol, deserves much of the credit.

Cover: General Andrew Jackson's ragtag army of Tennessee riflemen, New Orleans volunteers, and bayou pirates routs the pride of the British army at the Battle of New Orleans on January 8, 1815.

Maps by William J. Clipson

Cover photograph copyright ©: Historical Pictures Service, Chicago

Photographs copyright ©: New York Public Library, Picture Collection: pp. 2, 15, 26, 28, 32, 42, 45; North Wind Picture Archives, Alfred, ME: pp. 6, 10, 13, 21, 24, 36, 53 bottom, 56; The Olde Print Shop: p. 16; Anne S.K. Brown Military Collection, Brown University Library: pp. 33, 38; Peale Museum, Baltimore City Life Museums: p. 43; Bodo's Art Studio: p. 49 ("The Night Battle," by Sandor Bodo); National Museum of Art, Smithsonian Institution, Washington, DC: p. 53 top; West Point Museum Collections: p. 59.

Library of Congress Cataloging-in-Publication Data

Carter, Alden R.
The War of 1812 : second fight for independence / Alden R. Carter.
p.     cm.—(A First book)
Includes bibliographical references and index.
Summary: Discusses the causes, events, campaigns, personalities, and aftermath of the War of 1812.
ISBN 0-531-20080-9
1. United States—History—War of 1812—Juvenile literature.
[1. United States—History—War of 1812.]   I. Title.   II. Series.
E354.C37   1992
973.5'2—dc20                     92-11438   CIP   AC

# CONTENTS

# FREE TRADE AND SAILORS' RIGHTS

★

**S A I L S** full with a fresh summer wind, the USS *Chesapeake* cleared the harbor of Norfolk, Virginia, on June 22, 1807. Commodore James Barron gave orders setting course for the Mediterranean, then watched as his crew secured cannons and cargo for the long voyage ahead. The *Chesapeake* was a fine vessel, the product of America's genius for building fast, rugged, and handy ships. Rows of cannons, or broadsides, along its sides made the 38-gun frigate a match for any warship its size. But Barron did not expect to call on his ship's firepower this day. The United States was at peace, and he watched without concern as a British frigate approached.

HMS *Leopard* was one of the lesser ships of the British navy. While the United States Navy had only 17 ships—the largest not much bigger than the *Chesapeake*—the mighty Royal Navy had 119 "ships of the line" (the battleships of the time); 245 frigates (the cruisers); and hundreds of brigs and sloops (the destroyers).

Most of the Royal Navy was in European waters, protecting the home islands from an invasion by the French emperor Napoleon Bonaparte (1769–1821). Great Britain and France were locked in a great struggle. France had conquered most of continental Europe. Britain, protected by the narrow English Channel and its powerful navy, held out against the French tide.

The United States wanted no part in the latest war between the rival empires. In four wars between 1689 and 1763, American colonists had fought for Britain against the French and their Indian allies in Canada and the wilderness beyond the Appalachian Mountains. Victory in the Colonial Wars (also called the French and Indian wars) gave Britain control of North America. But France took revenge by helping the colonists win their independence during the American Revolution (1775–83). Wary of future European quarrels, the newly independent United States kept out of the fight when Britain and France resumed their long struggle less than a decade later.

Staying neutral was no easy task. Thousands of American merchant ships carried on a rich trade with Europe and the French and British islands of the Caribbean. America's economy depended on trading the harvest of its farms, fisheries, and forests for goods produced in European factories. American raw materials were vital to the war efforts of Britain and France, and both nations tried to deny the American trade to the other. They set strict rules in their ports and sent their navies to seize war materials bound for enemy ports on neutral ships. Lacking a large army and navy, the United States could only protest that neutral ships should be free to trade in any open port.

By 1807, British warships had largely destroyed the French navy outside European waters and could turn full attention to searching American ships for war supplies and deserters. Thousands of British sailors had escaped the cramped quarters, maggoty food, and dangerous duty on Royal Navy warships for the easier life aboard American merchant ships. Always shorthanded, British captains tried to discourage further desertions by capturing and hanging the renegades. To replace lost crewmen, they used impressment. Any British-born sailor found on an American ship—even if he held United States citizenship—was pressed into service. Many native-born Americans were taken by press gangs under orders to bring back able-bodied seamen whatever their citizenship. During the Napoleonic Wars, some 6,000 Americans were forced to serve in the Royal Navy.

Commodore Barron had seen British warships in action, but he expected no trouble as *Leopard* closed in on *Chesapeake*. The rules of search and impressment applied only to merchant ships. Warships treated each other politely, and he supposed that *Leopard*'s captain wanted him to carry letters to Europe. To his astonishment, *Leopard* signaled that it intended to send a boarding party to search

A British officer accuses an American sailor of being a deserter. About 6,000 American seamen were forced to serve aboard British warships during the Napoleonic Wars.

for deserters. Even facing *Leopard*'s ready cannons, Barron could not agree to this violation of international law and his country's honor. He gave rapid orders to clear decks for action, but an instant later the guns along *Leopard*'s side roared. One after another, three broadsides crashed into the helpless *Chesapeake*. With three American sailors dead and another eighteen wounded, Barron hauled down his flag. Marines from *Leopard* removed four sailors before allowing *Chesapeake* to limp back to port. One of the captured sailors was hung as a deserter, another died of illness, and the last two would wait four long years for freedom.

The *Chesapeake* Affair outraged the American people. President Thomas Jefferson (1743–1826) demanded an apology from Britain. The British government refused, issuing even stricter rules for American trade with continental Europe. The Orders in Council gave the Royal Navy the right to seize any neutral ship failing to dock for inspection in a British port. Napoleon struck back with the Milan Decree, ordering French port officials to seize any neutral ship that obeyed the British rules.

Unable to comply with both decrees at the same time and unwilling to bow to either, the United States cut off all trade with France and Britain. The Embargo Act of 1807 hurt America more than the warring nations. Thousands of sailors and dockworkers lost their jobs. Shipowners, farmers, tobacco planters, fishermen, lumbermen, and fur traders lost millions as American ships and cargoes lay rotting in port. The price of scarce European goods rose beyond the reach of most Americans. Desperate shippers risked ignoring British, French, and American rules. Lucky ships made huge profits, but some 900 American trading vessels were seized by Britain and France.

Jefferson left office in 1809 and was succeeded by James Madison (1751–1836). "Little Jemmy" Madison stood only five-feet-six (168 cm) and weighed barely 100 pounds (45 kg). Yet he was one of the giants among the founders of the United States. He had served in the Continental Congress during the Revolution, engineered the writing of the United States Constitution, taken a leading role in the House of Representatives, and helped arrange the purchase of the vast Louisiana Territory from France in 1803 as Jefferson's secretary of state. Reserved and soft-spoken in public, witty and earthy in private, Madison was brilliant, humane, and completely dedicated to the principles of republican government outlined in his beloved Constitution.

At Madison's request, Congress reopened trade with France and Britain in 1810. The lifting of the embargo contained a bribe: If either country removed restrictions on American trade, the United States would stop importing goods from the other. Napoleon quickly agreed, and Madison imposed nonimportation on British goods. The British government protested that Napoleon was lying and, in

President James Madison and First Lady Dolley Madison.
Although observers often commented on the contrast between
the reserved, almost fragile president and his outgoing wife, the
Madisons enjoyed a happy marriage of more than forty years.

truth, he was. But Madison held to his position. Relations between the United States and Britain went from bad to worse. Along the Atlantic Coast, Royal Navy and American warships taunted each other. On the night of May 16, 1811, the frigate USS *President* fired on the smaller HMS *Little Belt*, killing nine sailors and wounding twenty-three.

Trouble flared in the Old Northwest, the vast wilderness that would become the states of Ohio, Indiana, Illinois, Michigan, and Wisconsin. White settlers accused British officers in Canada of encouraging the Shawnee chief Tecumseh (c.1768–1813) in his plan to unite all the Native American tribes in a huge confederation. Tecumseh denied supporting Indian raids and tried to win fair treatment for his people in peace talks with Indiana's territorial governor, William Henry Harrison (1773–1841). They could not agree. Harrison's army marched into Shawnee territory while Tecumseh was visiting another tribe. Tecumseh's brother Tenskwatawa (the Prophet) gathered the warriors, promising them magical protection from white bullets. On November 7, 1811, the Indians attacked Harrison's camp near Prophet's Town on the Tippecanoe River in what is today northwestern Indiana. Although the Indians killed or wounded nearly 200 soldiers, 100 warriors fell to white bullets. The emptiness of Tenskwatawa's promise destroyed Tecumseh's confederation. Tecumseh fled north, vowing to carry on the fight from Canada.

With tension high at sea and on the frontier, Congress

USS *President* sends a devastating broadside into HMS *Little Belt*
on May 16, 1811. Hostile encounters between American and British
warships led to a war that neither nation could afford.

Peace talks between the great Shawnee chief Tecumseh and
Ohio's Governor William Henry Harrison explode in angry threats.
The failure of negotiations brought all-out war between whites
and Indians in the Old Northwest.

echoed with angry speeches: The British were stealing the hard-won independence of the United States. Without "free trade and sailors' rights," the country would become little more than a colony of Britain. The very future of government under the Constitution—indeed the future of republican government everywhere—hung by a thread. The United States must arm itself for "a second war of independence."

Madison tried to slow the rush toward war, but members of his own party led the charge. The Democratic-Republicans—or Democrats as they were later known—held majorities in both houses of Congress. Although united in calling for action, they split into factions over what plan to choose. Speaker of the House Henry Clay and his War Hawk faction of southern and western Democrats argued that the United States would never be safe until the British were driven from Canada. A second Democratic faction favored a naval war only. A third—the Scarecrow faction—thought that just declaring war would bluff the British into giving way to American demands.

The smaller but more unified Federalist party argued against war. The Federalists were strongest in New England, the center of America's shipping industry and the region with the most to lose in a complete breakdown of trade. The Federalists accused the Democrats, particularly the War Hawks, of being greedy schemers more interested in grabbing Canada than in solving America's problems with Britain by peaceful means.

The debate in Congress raged into the early months of 1812, while the peaceable Madison tried to negotiate a settlement with Britain. The British gave some ground. They would apologize for the *Chesapeake* Affair, release the two sailors still alive, ease tensions on the frontier, and order the Royal Navy from American coastal waters. In return, however, all American ships must apply for British trade licenses before sailing for continental Europe.

The license plan was an insult—one more British attempt to control American trade. Madison lost patience. On June 1, 1812, he sent a message to Congress listing the British offenses and concluding that Britain had all but declared war on the United States already. Congress began considering a declaration of war. On the far side of the Atlantic, the British government gave in to American complaints on June 16, junking the license plan, the Orders in Council, and all other restrictions on American shipping. The impressment issue remained, but with a little more patience, perhaps the two nations could reach a compromise. No one would ever know. On June 17, 1812—long before a ship could cross the Atlantic with news of the British concessions—Congress voted for war.

# BLUNDERS AND TRIUMPHS

**W A R** caught Americans by surprise. Most people had expected a peaceful solution to the troubles with Britain, and the War of 1812 quickly became one of the most unpopular wars in United States history.

The Federalists took the lead in criticizing the war. Pro-war mobs attacked Federalist newspaper offices, smashing presses and beating employees, but the Federalists refused to be silenced. In the Federalist Northeast, people talked of breaking away from the Union to make a separate peace with Britain. New England governors often refused to cooperate with the national government, claiming that states had the right to cancel—or "nullify"—laws made in Washington. Many Americans put profit ahead of patriotism. Farmers along the northern border traded with the British army in Canada. American ships carried supplies to the Royal Navy base at Halifax, Nova Scotia. All along the coast, Americans sold supplies to British ships arriving to blockade the nation's ports.

Madison himself was uncertain about the war. Like the Scarecrow faction of his party, he probably thought that a declaration of war would bluff the British into serious bargaining. Within days of the war's beginning, he sent friendly signals suggesting a peaceful settlement. But neither nation was yet willing to give way on the impressment issue.

The United States was almost completely unprepared for war. The army had only 12,000 men; the navy, only seventeen warships. Nor did the government have the money or machinery to build and manage a large military machine. The secretary of war's entire staff consisted of eleven inexperienced clerks. Nearly all government funds were collected in import taxes that were bound to plunge as the Royal Navy shut off America's sea trade.

A divided Congress and an uncertain president lurched ahead with preparations for the fighting to come. Congress licensed privateers—armed merchant vessels—to raid British shipping and offered bonuses of money and land to lure recruits into the army. The president asked the governors to call out their emergency defense troops—known as militia—for service in the national cause.

The United States needed a quick victory before Britain could send more ships and soldiers across the Atlantic. The vast, underpopulated wilderness of Canada seemed an

A cartoonist's view of a state militia company.
With only 12,000 regular soldiers at the outbreak
of war, the United States Army called on the
citizen soldiers of the militia to fill its ranks.

easy target. While the United States had a non-Indian
population of some 7,500,000, Canada had barely
500,000 people, and more than half were French Canadians with little love for their British rulers or the 7,000
British soldiers defending Canada's long border with the
United States. Former President Jefferson predicted that
taking Canada would be "just a matter of marching."

British rule in Canada depended on control of the water
route from the Great Lakes, along the St. Lawrence River,
to the ocean. President Madison approved a plan to cut the

waterway at three points. An American army from Ohio would march to Detroit and cross into Canada to break the link between Lake Erie and the western Great Lakes. In western New York, a second army would push the British from the Niagara River connecting lakes Erie and Ontario. In northeastern New York, a third army would march north along the shore of Lake Champlain to the St. Lawrence for an attack on Montreal. Success at Montreal would open the way for an attack on Canada's capital city of Quebec and an end to British rule in Canada.

On paper the plan made sense, but almost everything went wrong. The American armies were undermanned, poorly trained, and short of supplies. The generals were often politicians with little or no military experience. State militias refused to cross into Canada, announcing that they would fight only to protect American soil.

The British took advantage of every American weakness. In the West, the daring General Sir Isaac Brock rallied Canadian militia and Tecumseh's Indians. When General William Hull's American army of 2,000 crossed into Canada from Detroit in early July 1812, Brock cut its supply lines. Hull lost his nerve and retreated to Detroit. Brock followed with his 300 regulars, 400 militia, and 600 Indians. He called on the Americans to surrender, warning that his *5,000* unruly Indians were planning a massacre. Over his officers' protests, Hull surrendered on August 16.

The loss of Detroit was only the beginning of the bad

news to reach Washington. Deep in the wilderness, the British captured the unsuspecting American garrison at Fort Mackinac in the vital strait between lakes Huron and Michigan. At Chicago, where Fort Dearborn guarded the short portage connecting Lake Michigan with the Mississippi River system, Indians slaughtered the fleeing American garrison. On the Niagara River, two rival American generals squabbled away an overwhelming advantage in numbers. Brock's tiny army threw back an American attack at Queens Town, Ontario, on October 13, killing 300 and capturing 950 regulars who waited in vain for militiamen who refused to cross the border. The victory cost the British only 100 casualties, but among the dead lay the gallant General Isaac Brock.

The American advance up Lake Champlain toward Montreal did not even begin until mid-November. With the threat of winter on the wind, General Henry Dearborn retreated after a single skirmish with British regulars. A disgusted newspaper editor summed up the United States Army's efforts in 1812 as "an unbroken series of disaster, defeat, disgrace . . . ruin, and death."

Fortunately for America, the opposite was true at sea. The small United States Navy had only eight frigates and nine smaller brigs and sloops, but they were superbly designed ships manned by courageous officers and expert crews. The war was only three days old when Commodore John Rodgers sailed from New York with a powerful Amer-

Gunners cheer as USS *Constitution* goes into action.
America's fast, heavily armed warships proved more than a
match for the mighty Royal Navy in the first year of the war.

ican squadron. Rodgers hoped to pick off the widely scattered ships of Vice Admiral Herbert Sawyer's British squadron based at Halifax.

Sawyer was struggling with an impossible list of duties. With only one ship of the line, nine frigates, and twenty-seven smaller vessels, he was supposed to blockade the American coast, hunt down privateers, and escort merchant convoys. The news that Rodgers was at sea forced Sawyer to gather his ships for battle. The squadrons missed each other in the wide reaches of the Atlantic, but Rodgers had frustrated Sawyer's plan for a blockade. Hundreds of American merchant ships reached home safely while a swarm of privateers put out to sea. In the next six months American privateers would capture 450 British merchant ships.

Still looking for Rodgers, Sawyer dispatched his ships one at a time to resupply in Halifax. Sailing north on August 19, HMS *Guerrière*, a large 49-gun frigate, ran into a lone American frigate sailing from Boston, the USS *Constitution*. Fast and maneuverable, with a hull of oak, and carrying 54 guns, *Constitution* was perhaps the deadliest frigate afloat. The two ships closed to within "half a pistol shot"—about 10 yards (9 m)—and pounded each other with broadsides. One of *Guerrière*'s masts toppled over the side, its dragging sail slowing the ship. *Constitution* swung across *Guerrière*'s bow to deliver a broadside that swept the length of its decks. Coming about, *Constitu-*

The USS *Constitution*, perhaps the deadliest
frigate afloat, batters HMS *Guerrière*
into surrender on August 19, 1812.

*tion* raked *Guerrière* again. *Guerrière* lay rolling help-lessly, its remaining masts shot away, its hold filling with water, and its decks littered with dead and wounded. The British captain lowered his flag.

With night falling, American sailors helped their Brit-ish cousins transfer the wounded from the sinking *Guer-rière* to the *Constitution*. Sometime in the hush after battle, men recalled how cannonballs had bounced off *Constitu-tion*'s oak sides. Nicknamed "Old Ironsides," the *Consti-tution* would become the most famous ship in the navy's history.

America greeted news of *Constitution*'s triumph with wild celebration. Opposition to the war quieted with re-ports of yet more American victories at sea: the frigate *Essex* over the brig HMS *Alert*; the sloop *Wasp* over the sloop HMS *Frolic*; the frigate *United States* over the frigate HMS *Macedonian*; the *Constitution* again, this time over the frigate HMS *Java*; and finally, in late February 1813, the sloop *Hornet* over the sloop HMS *Peacock*. Unfor-tunately, the American victories worked against an early end to the war. The success of the upstart United States Navy broke a decade-long string of victories by the Royal Navy. Shocked and outraged, the British public howled for revenge.

In the early months of 1813, Britain sent large re-inforcements to North America. Dozens of British war-ships joined the blockade, closing harbors and bottling the

Boats from the USS *Constitution* rescue sailors
from the burning HMS *Guerrière*. Recalling how
cannonballs bounced off the *Constitution*'s hull, a sailor
gave the frigate its nickname, "Old Ironsides."

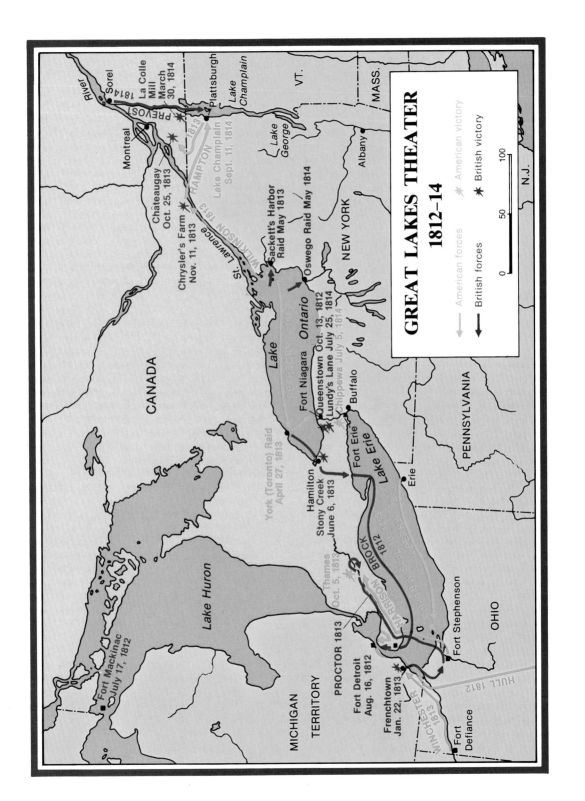

GREAT LAKES THEATER
1812–14

American forces
British forces
American victory
British victory

0    50    100

CANADA

Lake Huron

Fort Mackinac
July 17, 1812

MICHIGAN
TERRITORY

PROCTOR 1813

Fort Detroit
Aug. 16, 1812

Thames
Oct. 5, 1813

Frenchtown
Jan. 22, 1813

Fort
Defiance

HARRISON 1813

BROCK 1812

Fort Stephenson

OHIO

HULL 1813

WINCHESTER 1813

Lake Erie

Erie

PENNSYLVANIA

York (Toronto) Raid
April 27, 1813

Hamilton
Stony Creek
June 6, 1813

Fort Erie

Buffalo

Chippewa July 5, 1814
Lundy's Lane July 25, 1814
Queenstown Oct. 13, 1812

Fort Niagara

Lake Ontario

Sackett's Harbor
Raid May 1813

Oswego Raid May 1814

NEW YORK

Albany

Chrysler's Farm
Nov. 11, 1813

WILKINSON 1813

St. Lawrence

Châteauguay
Oct. 25, 1813

Montreal

PREVOST

Sorel

River

La Colle
Mill
March
30, 1814

1814

1813

HAMPTON 1813

Lake Champlain
Sept. 11, 1814

Plattsburgh

Lake Champlain

Lake
George

VT.

MASS.

N.J.

United States Navy in port. Trade and tax collections plunged. Prices skyrocketed. Federalist politicians and newspapers screamed for an end to the war. New England talked openly of making a separate peace.

For all his other talents, President Madison lacked the powerful personality needed to unite Congress and the people behind the war. In frail health and anxious for peace, he quickly accepted a Russian offer to arrange a settlement. But the British were no longer interested in an early peace; they intended to punish America first. In March, a British fleet entered Chesapeake Bay to begin nine months of raiding. Landing parties found little opposition as they burned town after town in Maryland and Virginia. To balance the damage on Chesapeake Bay, the American army needed to win on the Canadian border. The army was improving with experience, better organization, and thousands of fresh recruits. The new secretary of war, John Armstrong, laid out a plan to regain the offensive.

British ships controlled Lakes Erie and Ontario, making movement of American troops and supplies very difficult. The Americans began building fleets on the lakes. Most of the effort went into the Lake Ontario–Niagara River front. The British matched the Americans ship for ship and raid for raid, with neither side holding the upper hand for long.

On Lake Erie, a young naval officer named Oliver

Hazard Perry (1785–1819) took charge of the American fleet under construction at Presque Isle (today's Erie), Pennsylvania. He raced against time as General William Henry Harrison's outnumbered American army clung to a string of forts on the southwestern edge of the lake. Perry's shipbuilders worked furiously through the summer of 1813 under constant threat of attack by Captain Robert Barclay's British squadron. By late August, Perry had two 20-gun ships and seven small schooners ready for action. Perry named his flagship for Captain James Lawrence, whose unlucky frigate *Chesapeake* had been overpowered by a heavier British frigate off Boston that spring. Stitched on Perry's battle flag were Lawrence's dying words: *Don't give up the ship*.

On September 10, the evenly matched fleets met at Put-in-Bay on the western end of the lake. Perry rushed in with the *Lawrence*, but his second in command held the 20-gun *Niagara* back, trying to score hits at long range. Alone against Barclay's two large ships, *Detroit* and *Queen Charlotte*, the *Lawrence* took a frightful pounding. With 80 percent of his crew dead or wounded, Perry leaped aboard a boat and was rowed through a hail of fire to the *Niagara*. He took command and steered back into battle. Trying to maneuver, *Detroit* and *Queen Charlotte* collided. *Niagara*'s broadsides raked their decks. With Barclay terribly wounded, the British gave up the fight.

Perry's ships ferried Harrison's 5,500 men across the

Abandoning his crippled flagship for another warship,
Commodore Oliver Hazard Perry points the way through
a storm of fire at the Battle of Lake Erie.

General William Henry Harrison's cavalry shatters the British
and Indian ranks at the Battle of the Thames. Tecumseh, the greatest
Native American leader of his generation, died in the fighting.

lake as the British army retreated east from Detroit. Harrison caught them on October 5 at the Battle of the Thames. A charge by 1,200 Kentucky horsemen shattered the British and Indian ranks. Tecumseh, the greatest Native American leader of his generation, was killed, his warriors scattered, and nearly all the British regulars captured. The Americans had retaken the Old Northwest.

The Americans also seemed poised for a great victory farther east as two American armies—one sailing east from Lake Ontario, the other marching north from Lake Champlain—prepared to attack Montreal. But the commanders were personal enemies and could not agree on a plan. The British whipped them separately at Châteauguay in Quebec on October 25, and at Chrysler's Farm in Ontario on November 11. The twin defeats opened a season of terror and death along the northern border.

The American army on the Niagara frontier had lost most of its strength to the ill-fated expedition against Montreal. In December, the Americans withdrew to their side of the river, leaving the Canadian village of Newark in ashes and its people freezing in the subzero cold. Outraged, the British commander in the area ordered a terrible revenge. His Indian allies crossed the river to burn and kill the length of the American shore. On December 30, 1813, 1,400 British regulars stormed into Buffalo and nearby Black Rock to put both towns to the torch. It was a fate soon to be shared by the American capital itself.

# 1814
# THE CRISIS

**T H E  C L I M A X** of more than twenty years of war in Europe came in the spring of 1814. The armies of Britain and its allies marched into France. With his armies destroyed and his enemies hammering at the gates of Paris, Napoleon surrendered on April 11. He would escape from exile for a final stand at the Battle of Waterloo in 1815, but for the moment, Britain could turn its attention to the war across the Atlantic. Thousands of battle-hardened regulars boarded ships for America to whip the upstart Yankees and force a peace that would clip the wings of the American eagle for good.

In early July, British forces landed in Maine, seizing 100 miles (160 km) of coastline between the Penobscot and St. Croix rivers. On the Niagara frontier, British reinforcements turned back the last American attempt to invade Canada at the Battle of Lundy's Lane on July 25. A month later the British struck at the American capital. A British fleet sailed into Chesapeake Bay to land 4,500

regulars under General Robert Ross at Benedict, Maryland, on August 19.

Washington panicked. There were no defenses and few regular troops to defend the city. General William Winder managed to gather 1,000 regulars and 6,000 militia for a stand at Bladensburg, Maryland, 5 miles (8 km) from the city. The British arrived early in the afternoon of August 24 to find the Americans drawn up in three ragged lines. The British regulars attacked with all their famed bravery and skill. The American lines crumpled, the militia fleeing in what British veterans laughingly called the "Bladensburg Races."

About the coolest head in Washington that afternoon belonged to the president's energetic wife. Dolley Madison (1768–1849) directed the loading of government records and the White House valuables. According to legend, she carried a portrait of President Washington in her arms when she left the White House for safety in the countryside. The British marched into Washington that evening. British officers dined in the White House on the Madisons' uneaten supper, took some souvenirs, then set the building on fire. Before long the Capitol building, the treasury, the navy yard, and the war and state department building were

British warships blockade Chesapeake Bay.
Britain's victory over Napoleon
in 1814 freed scores of ships
and thousands of battle-hardened
soldiers for service in North America.

After routing American militia at the Battle
of Bladensburg, Maryland, British troops burn
Washington, D.C., on the night of August 24, 1814.

also in flames. The British withdrew to the coast the next day, leaving official Washington in ashes.

The government crept back into the city. Madison and his cabinet set up offices in private homes. Secretary of War Armstrong resigned, his duties taken by Secretary of State James Monroe (1758–1831). But with the British fleet in control of the Chesapeake, there was little the government could do to turn the tide of war. That task fell to the people of Baltimore.

The Royal Navy held a grudge against Baltimore, a pro-war hotbed and the home port for scores of privateers. Admiral Sir Alexander Cochrane swore that he would clean out the nest of "pirates." His plan called for Ross's army to attack the city by land while the fleet battered its way past Fort McHenry to shell the city from the harbor. The Marylanders dared the British to attack. Thousands of men, women, and children turned out to dig earthworks to protect Baltimore. Senator Samuel Smith, a militia general, manned the fortifications with more than 10,000 raw but willing volunteers.

Ross's army landed at North Point, 14 miles (22.5 km) from Baltimore, on September 12. Marching toward the city, the redcoats ran into Maryland militia sent to delay their advance. From the cover of Godly Wood, the Americans delivered a punishing fire as they withdrew slowly toward the city. Two young militiamen lagging a little behind spotted a British officer on a white horse riding

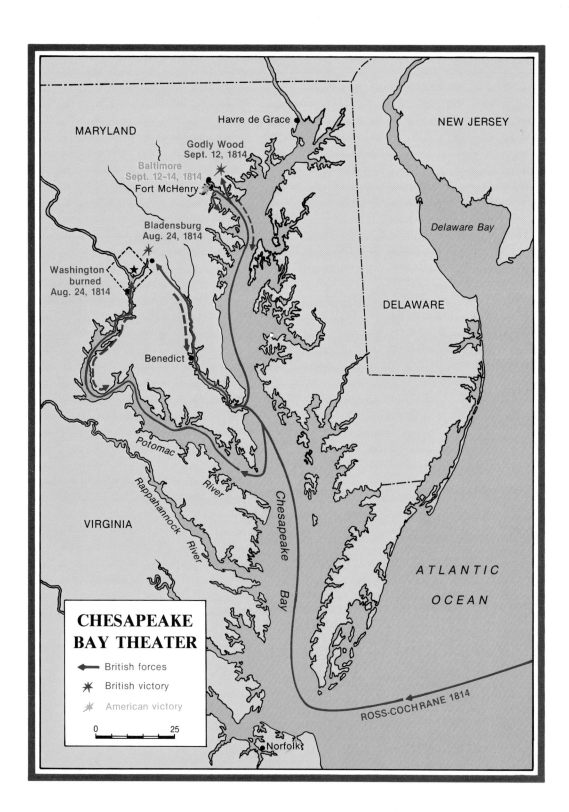

MARYLAND

Havre de Grace

Godly Wood
Sept. 12, 1814

Baltimore
Sept. 12–14, 1814

Fort McHenry

Bladensburg
Aug. 24, 1814

Washington
burned
Aug. 24, 1814

Benedict

NEW JERSEY

Delaware Bay

DELAWARE

Potomac
River

Rappahannock
River

Chesapeake Bay

VIRGINIA

ATLANTIC
OCEAN

ROSS-COCHRANE 1814

Norfolk

**CHESAPEAKE
BAY THEATER**

British forces

British victory

American victory

0        25

forward to view the ground ahead. They aimed their squirrel rifles and shot General Ross from the saddle. Charging redcoats killed the boys, then returned to weep over the body of their beloved general. Ross's second in command led the column forward but halted at the sight of Baltimore's bristling defenses.

British success now depended on the navy blasting its way into the harbor. Cochrane's ships began bombarding Fort McHenry at sunrise on September 13. Unable to reply with their shorter-range guns, the 1,000 Americans inside huddled under the cover of the fort's stout walls. The British fired all day and on into the night. Francis Scott Key (1779–1843), a Baltimore lawyer detained aboard one of Cochrane's ships, watched anxiously for the flash of an exploding shell or the fiery arc of a rocket to show him if the American flag still flew defiantly on the fort's ramparts. It was still there in the dawn, inspiring Key to write the words that would become the national anthem of the United States: "The Star-Spangled Banner." That afternoon a frustrated Cochrane gave up the attack.

The British fleet sailed for Jamaica to make repairs. Rejoicing Americans soon had word of another great victory, this one on the waters of Lake Champlain. For more than a century, armies had fought to control the long, narrow lake forming the natural invasion route from Montreal on the St. Lawrence to New York City at the mouth of the Hudson River. In late August 1814, Sir George

Shells explode over Fort McHenry as the British
fleet tries to force its way into Baltimore
harbor on the night of September 13, 1814.

By the dawn's early light on September 14, 1814,
Francis Scott Key sees the American flag waving
defiantly from the ramparts of Fort McHenry.
Key celebrated the American victory with his
poem "The Star-Spangled Banner."

Prevost, the governor-general of Canada, set out with 10,000 men to try the ancient route again. Prevost expected little trouble beating the 3,400 Americans blocking his way at Plattsburgh, New York, but he worried about the American naval squadron on the lake. Most of his army's supplies traveled by water, and he could not risk marching too far south while American ships threatened his supply lines. On September 6, Prevost halted his army within sight of the Plattsburgh defenses to wait for the naval squadron of Captain George Downie.

In Plattsburgh harbor, Lieutenant Thomas Macdonough (1783–1825) prepared his American ships for action. Like Perry on Lake Erie, Macdonough had built his small fleet from practically nothing. His four ships and ten gunboats had about the same firepower as Downie's squadron, but the Americans had fewer of the long-range guns needed for a successful fight on the open waters of the lake. Macdonough decided to stay in the protected harbor, where Downie would have to fight at close range. He anchored his ships bow and stern so that they could swing around in the heat of battle to fire undamaged broadsides.

The British ships sailed boldly into Plattsburgh harbor on the morning of September 11. As the gunboats and small ships rushed in to engage Macdonough's light vessels, Downie's flagship the *Confiance* (37 guns) and the *Linnet* (16 guns) anchored to slug it out with the American flagship *Saratoga* (26 guns) and the *Eagle* (20 guns). The

Luring the British fleet into the narrow harbor
of Plattsburgh Bay, New York, Lieutenant Thomas
Macdonough's American squadron opens a deadly
fire at the Battle of Lake Champlain.

heavier British fire caused terrible casualties on the American ships. The severed head of one crewman knocked down Macdonough. He stumbled to his feet, dazed but still in control. He directed a deadly counterfire that killed Downie and nearly all the officers aboard *Confiance*.

First *Eagle*, then *Saratoga* swung around to fire their undamaged broadsides. The junior lieutenant left in command of *Confiance* tried to imitate the American trick. Unprepared for the difficult maneuver, *Confiance* swung too slowly. *Saratoga*'s guns raked *Confiance*, killing or wounding nearly everyone above deck. The surviving sailors abandoned their guns. Under the overwhelming fire of both *Saratoga* and *Eagle*, *Linnet* gave up. Only a few British gunboats escaped. Prevost's soldiers gave up the attack on Plattsburgh, shouldered their packs, and began the long trudge back to Canada.

The American victories on Lake Champlain and at Baltimore changed the course of the war. After the long struggle with Napoleon, the British people were sick of high taxes, high prices, and the waste of so many young lives. The political balance in Europe was delicate, and the great Duke of Wellington, the conqueror of Napoleon, advised against a long war in far-off America. The British government listened and decided to give up trying to force a harsh peace on the United States.

In Ghent, Belgium, British and American representatives at last began serious talks to end the war. The American negotiators dropped the impressment question—already a dead issue with the end of the European wars—then skillfully outmaneuvered the British on nearly every other issue. After haggling for a few weeks, both sides agreed to restore borders to pre-war lines. On December 24, they signed the Treaty of Ghent. The British government quickly approved the treaty. On January 2, 1815, HMS *Favourite* sailed for America with a copy for ratification by the Senate and signature by the president. But even the fast-sailing *Favourite* needed forty days to cross the Atlantic. In the delay a motley band of Americans destroyed a proud British army at New Orleans in the most famous battle of the war.

In 1814, New Orleans was the richest city in America. Its docks groaned under the weight of cotton, tobacco, and corn barged down the Mississippi for transfer to seagoing ships. Part of the United States only since the Louisiana Purchase of 1803, the city had no deep loyalty to the republic. Its people—a mixture of French, Spanish, English, Caribbean, and African cultures—went their colorful, independent way, paying little attention to the war.

On December 1, 1814, General Andrew Jackson (1767–1845) rode into New Orleans determined to cure the city of its careless attitude. As military commander of Mississippi Territory, Jackson had crushed the Creek Indians, Britain's allies along the Georgia border, and driven the British from their base at Pensacola in Spanish-owned

**NEW ORLEANS CAMPAIGN    1814–15**

← American forces         American victory

← British forces          British victory

0    50    100

Fort Jackson

JACKSON 1814

Fort Claiborne

MISSISSIPPI

Fort Mims

LOUISIANA

Dec. 14, 1814

JACKSON 1814

Mobile

TERRITORY

SPANISH   FLORIDA

GEORGIA

Mississippi

River

Fort Bowyer
Sept. 15, 1814

Pensacola

NICHOLLS
1814

New Orleans
Jan. 8, 1815

1815

Fort St. Philip

1814 COCHRANE-PAKENHAM (from JAMAICA)

GULF OF MEXICO

JACKSON

AMERICAN LINE

Mississippi River

HIGHLANDERS

MAIN
FORCE

PAKENHAM

**BATTLE OF NEW ORLEANS**

Trying to slow the British advance
on New Orleans, General Andrew Jackson
leads a night attack on December 23, 1814.

Florida. He expected the British to strike back with an attack on New Orleans. Jackson energized the city with a mixture of charm and threats. Thousands of volunteers, black and white alike, joined Jackson's small army of regulars and Tennessee riflemen. Jean Laffite (c.1780– c.1826), the pirate king of the Louisiana bayous, sent cannons and skilled gunners to help defend the city.

The British arrived in mid-December. Admiral Cochrane's fleet ferried 7,500 veterans of Wellington's army to the shores of Lake Borgne southeast of New Orleans. Slowed by swamps, terrible weather, and night raids by the Americans, the British pushed forward until they reached the McCarty plantation 7 miles (11.3 km) below the city. There they found Jackson's strange little army drawn up behind a log-and-earthen wall running across a low, wet field. With a swamp on the right and the Mississippi on the left, the only way through was a direct attack into the teeth of the American guns. General Sir Edward Pakenham ordered his proud veterans forward on the morning of January 8. It was murder. The concentrated American musket and cannon fire stacked Wellington's "invincibles" in scarlet heaps. In half an hour the Americans killed, wounded, or captured more than half of the attacking force of 4,000 men. American losses were 13 killed and 58 wounded. The British retreated to the sea, the last foreign army ever to invade America.

# AMERICA LOOKS WEST

**THE** *FAVOURITE* docked in New York on February 11, 1815. The peace treaty was rushed to Washington, where it was quickly approved by the Senate and signed by the president on February 17. It took time for the news of peace to spread. For months after, American and British merchant ships, privateers, and warships continued to run, hide, and fight on the ocean. Cruising in the South Pacific, the American sloop *Peacock* fired the last shots of the war on June 30.

The war ended in a military draw. Official records listed 2,260 Americans killed and 4,505 wounded. Historians estimate another 17,000 died of disease or accidents. British casualties were roughly equal. Although neither side gained territory or advantage in the war, Britain and the rest of Europe at last recognized that the American republic was not a weak alliance of states but a unified nation with a lasting place in the world. Although occasionally at odds, Britain and the United States would never fight again. In the twentieth century they would become firm friends.

After the War of 1812, the United States gave up any thought of conquering Canada and turned instead to the challenges of settling the Old Northwest and opening the great wilderness beyond the Mississippi. North of the border, Canadians built their nation in an era free from the fear of invasion. Today Canada and the United States share the longest undefended border in the world.

In the years following the Treaty of Ghent, Americans forgot how close they had come to losing the fight and began to view the war as a glorious page in the nation's history. The Democratic party became even more popular, while the Federalist party all but disappeared within a decade. In a political "Era of Good Feelings," the Democrats adopted many sound Federalist ideas on putting the nation's finances in order, preventing illegal trade, and providing for a stronger defense.

In many ways the War of 1812 was a second war for independence—a fight not against foreign rule but against the limitations of the past. Americans felt a new self-confidence and sense of national purpose as they pushed westward. There would be both glory and tragedy in the settlement of the West. The wave of development would destroy great forests, vast herds of buffalo, and the proud, free life of the American Indian. Argument over the spread

Peace negotiators exchange copies of the Treaty of Ghent. Although Britain and the United States would remain rivals for decades, they would never fight again.

Following the War of 1812, Americans and Canadians alike turned westward to face the challenge of settling the wilderness.

of slavery into the new lands would tear the nation apart and lead to the American Civil War, in which single battles would cost more American lives than the entire War of 1812.

Through good times and bad, the nation could depend on the principles of republican government written and preserved by James Madison and his generation. Madison left office in 1817. Four of the next five presidents were men who had served him well in the War of 1812: Secretary of State James Monroe, peace negotiator John Quincy Adams, General Andrew Jackson, and General William Henry Harrison. For the last twenty years of his long life, Madison lent his quiet wisdom to the nation. Madison had not been a forceful wartime president, but even in the worst moments of the fight, he had refused to set aside the Constitution and its promise of free and open government by the people. As the Constitution had escaped the flames of a burning Washington in 1814, the great principles it stated would survive every challenge down through the decades to our time.

# WARSHIPS IN THE AGE OF SAIL

**THE WARSHIPS** of the eighteenth and early nineteenth centuries came in a wide variety of sizes and designs. Ships of the line were the battleships of the era. The smallest carried 64 guns and a crew of about 500, the largest as many as 120 guns and a crew of nearly 1,000. Most of the great sea battles of the Napoleonic Wars were fought between huge fleets of British and French ships of the line sailing in parallel columns. The United States had no ships of the line in the War of 1812, and the British could spare only a few for the fight in American waters.

Frigates were the cruisers of the day. They blockaded enemy ports, scouted for the fleet, escorted convoys, and hunted enemy frigates, privateers, and merchant ships. The smallest had some 30 guns and a crew of 200. The largest—like the famous American frigate *Constitution*—carried as many as 56 guns and a crew of more than 400.

Quarters were tight, food poor, and the work long and dangerous aboard a warship. Yet many sailors served from childhood to old age rather than seek an easier life ashore.

In single combat, the fine frigates of the small United States Navy were usually more than a match for British frigates.

Sloops and brigs were the most common of the small seagoing ships in both navies. Mounting 16 to 24 guns and carrying a crew of about 150, they scouted, carried messages, chased enemy merchant ships, and fought their own kind. In coastal waters and inland lakes, even small schooners and gunboats, mounting from 1 to 10 guns, carried troops and supplies, raided, and fought on the outskirts of battles between larger ships.

The muzzle-loading cannons of the time were rated according to the weight of the solid iron ball they fired. As well as solid shot, cannons could fire chain shot to cut sails and rigging or deadly loads of small balls called grapeshot to kill sailors on the decks of enemy ships. Ships of the line and large frigates carried 32-pounders as their main armament. Light frigates, sloops, and brigs carried 24- or 12-pounders.

Combat between two ships usually started with a long chase as the ships maneuvered for the best position while trading shots with bow and stern guns. When one captain gained the advantage of the wind, he closed to within 50 yards (45 m) or less. The two ships pounded each other with broadsides: the fire of all the cannons on their facing sides. Half or more of the crews could be killed or wounded in these savage exchanges. As the damage mounted, the captain of the weaker ship might try to close the distance until the ships collided and his surviving sailors and marines could leap aboard the other ship for a desperate hand-to-hand fight. But this boarding maneuver took both skill and a great deal of luck. More often the decisive moment in a fight came when the less damaged ship managed to pull ahead, then turned across the bow of its opponent. This put the faster ship in position to deliver a deadly raking fire that swept the length of the other's decks, a tactic that usually forced a quick surrender.

# THE FLINTLOCK MUSKET

**S O L D I E R S** on both sides in the War of 1812 depended on the flintlock musket. Five feet (1.5 m) long and weighing 10 pounds (4.5 kg), the British Brown Bess fired a lead ball weighing more than 1 ounce (28 g). Although accurate only to about 75 yards (67.5 m), it was a deadly weapon in the hands of infantrymen firing in tight ranks.

An expert could load and fire three or four shots a minute. Each soldier carried paper-wrapped ammunition in a cartridge pouch slung at his side. To load his weapon, he tore the end of a cartridge with his teeth, sprinkled gunpowder into the pan of the firing mechanism, and then rammed the rest of the cartridge down the barrel with a long steel rod called a ramrod. Aiming his musket, the soldier pulled the trigger. A piece of flint on the falling hammer created a spark when it slapped back the steel latch covering the firing pan. The spark ignited the powder in the pan,

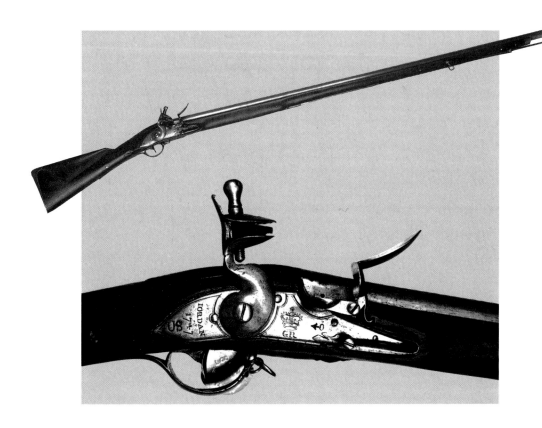

which in turn set off the powder charge in the barrel, driving the ball out to hit—or more likely miss—the target.

Rifles gained popularity during the war. Unlike smooth-bore muskets, rifle barrels had a spiral groove that put a spin on the bullet, increasing both range and accuracy. Rifles, however, took longer to load because of the extra effort needed to ram tight-fitting bullets.

# SUGGESTED READING

Buehr, Walter. *1812: The War and the World*. Chicago: Rand McNally, 1967.

Forester, C. S. *The Age of Fighting Sail*. New York: Doubleday, 1958.

Goldston, Robert. *The Battles of the* Constitution. New York: Macmillan, 1969.

Hickey, Donald R. *The War of 1812: A Forgotten Conflict*. Urbana: University of Illinois Press, 1989.

Marrin, Albert. *1812: The War Nobody Won*. New York: Atheneum, 1985.

Steinberg, Alfred. *James Madison*. New York: G. P. Putnam's Sons, 1965.

# INDEX

## ABOUT THE AUTHOR

**A L D E N   R.   C A R T E R** is a versatile writer for children and young adults. He has written nonfiction books on electronics, supercomputers, radio, Illinois, Shoshoni Indians, the People's Republic of China, the Alamo, the Battle of Gettysburg, the Colonial Wars, the Mexican-American War, the Civil War, the Spanish-American War, and five books on the American Revolution—*The American Revolution: War for Independence, Colonies in Revolt, Darkest Hours, At the Forge of Liberty,* and *Birth of the Republic.* His novels *Growing Season* (1984), *Wart, Son of Toad* (1985), *Sheila's Dying* (1987), and *Up Country* (1989) were named to the American Library Association's annual list, Best Books for Young Adults. His fifth novel, *RoboDad,* was honored as Best Children's Fiction Book of 1990 by the Society of Midland Authors. Mr. Carter lives with his wife, Carol, and their children, Brian Patrick and Siri Morgan, in Marshfield, Wisconsin.